Run to the Roar

A Fable of Choice, Courage and Hope

Run to the Roar

A Fable of Choice, Courage and Hope

J. RANDY FORBES
with contributions by
ROLFE CARAWAN

New York

Run to the Roar

A Fable of Choice, Courage and Hope

Disclaimer: The Publisher and the Author make no representations or warranties with respect to the accuracy or completeness of the contents of this work and specifically disclaim all warranties, including without limitation warranties of fitness for a particular purpose. No warranty may be created or extended by sales or promotional materials. The advice and strategies contained herein may not be suitable for every situation. This work is sold with the understanding that the Publisher is not engaged in rendering legal, accounting, or other professional services. If professional assistance is required, the services of a competent professional person should be sought. Neither the Publisher nor the Author shall be liable for damages arising herefrom. The fact that an organization or website is referred to in this work as a citation and/or a potential source of further information does not mean that the Author or the Publisher endorses the information the organization or website may provide or recommendations it may make. Further, readers should be aware that internet websites listed in this work may have changed or disappeared between when this work was written and when it is read.

ISBN 978-1-60037-604-7

Library of Congress Control Number: 2009905366

Cover Design by: Tony Laidig
                  www.thecoverexpert.com
                  tony@thecoverexpert.com

MORGAN · JAMES
THE ENTREPRENEURIAL PUBLISHER
Morgan James Publishing, LLC
1225 Franklin Ave., STE 325
Garden City, NY 11530-1693
Toll Free 800-485-4943
www.MorganJamesPublishing.com

The sun was breaking the announcement of a new day's birth to the rest of the world. Leeder walked confidently through the lush grassland that seemed to stretch endlessly before him, alternating between sniffing the luxurious grass and extending his neck in an attempt to see above it. The rains had passed leaving the grass tender and green with the air so invigorating that to breathe seemed like one of nature's desserts.

Leeder had always felt there was something special about this time of day. It was as if those who were disciplined enough to wake up and enjoy it were somehow rewarded with a preview of the world before it was officially open for business.

Yet most of the vast herd of antelope, zebra, and rhinos who had bedded down in the grassland the previous evening were content to savor their last moments of rest before the sun's heat compelled them to resume their daily routine of grazing.

The enormous thicket of trees to the south of the herd was starting to come alive from the top down. The birds filled the trees with a tapestry of sound as arousing as the smell of morning coffee, issuing a call to begin the process of life yet once more.

With each new step Leeder took, the treetops from the thicket were growing smaller in the background as land does to a ship sailing towards the horizon. The warmth of the sun made his muscles feel so alive that he felt driven to jump, run, and keep moving forward. He paused to sip from one of the newly formed watering holes not because he was thirsty, but rather because life seemed so good that he wanted to drink it all in.

He gazed at his reflection in the shimmering water and made no attempt to mask the pride in what he saw. His coat was a beautiful reddish caramel, darker on top than the bottom, and it was free of the cuts and scars he saw on many of the other antelope. He had filled out much during the last year, and the image he saw flickering in the water confirmed the quiet strength he was now feeling inside. But perhaps it was the increased growth of his horns that made him feel his newfound manhood most of all.

As he trotted further away from the thicket, Leeder felt a twinge of doubt. Since birth, he had understood the importance of staying with the herd. It was never spoken of or openly taught, but it was something all the antelope just knew. Staying with the herd was always safer and gave a sense of belonging.

His entire education about life had evolved from watching and imitating the herd. When they moved, he moved. When they drank, he drank. When they ate, he ate. He never thought about whether it was a good system or a bad system. It was the only system. And it had served him well.

But not today. Today, for the first time, he was in the vast grassland alone and away from the herd. His stomach churned as he took each new step. The smell of freedom and the sense of independence mixed with a fear of the unknown, made him feel alive and afraid at the same time.

He kicked the air. Not because he needed to, but just because it felt good. He ran. He stopped. He turned. He snorted. And then he began to roll in the soft grass which seemed like a giant blanket wrapping him in warmth and security.

As quickly as he began his first roll, however, he sensed a movement coming toward him, parting the tall sea of grass like a torpedo on a mission with him as the target. The adrenaline of fear overtook every other thought or feeling and instinctively propelled him in the air, kicking his hind legs frantically without aim. Just as abruptly as it started, however, the torpedo came to a sliding stop amidst a cloud of grass and dust from which a deep voice cried out, "Whoa little buddy! Did I scare you or something?"

Leeder sighed with relief as he looked into the familiar face of his friend, big 'C.'

"You big oaf, of course you scared me! I thought you were one of the Killers. I could have hurt you!" Leeder anxiously exclaimed.

With that statement, big 'C' literally fell to the ground holding his stomach as he rolled back and forth. Through his deep and barreling laugh he managed to utter, "You hurt me? You hurt me? And just when were you going to do that, before or after your legs stopped trembling?"

Leeder and 'C' had known each other since birth and had become almost inseparable. 'C' was a short, stocky rhino with multiple humps on his back, large pig-like ears, and two horns located one behind the other. The longer horn was massive and often the brunt of many good-natured jokes. His legs were short and seemed out of proportion to his huge body. He looked like muscle that had been bred to rock, and Leeder always felt his friend should have been named Rocky.

However, 'C's parents had stuck the rather stuffy name Courage to the big fellow. Leeder refused to call him that primarily because he felt it would make him conceited, so the nickname 'Big C' or 'C' for short was branded to him by their circle of friends.

Just as Leeder was gaining enough composure to keep his voice from trembling so he could resume yelling at 'C,' he once again found himself startled and leaping high in the air with his legs kicking aimlessly as a voice from behind him said, "He's a little jumpy today, isn't he 'C'? I'd be careful around those wild legs if I were you. He looks mighty dangerous."

As Leeder came to the ground, he saw an attractive female antelope laughing as she made her way through the field of grass. Faith was quieter than most of Leeder's other friends, and he had known her all his life. She was soft-spoken, and her every word was full of hope and assurance. She also had the kindest eyes Leeder had ever seen.

'C' was the one always ready to tackle anything. Despite his size, he was tremendously quick. Not fast, but quick. In short races he would consistently take the lead, but his short legs and large body would soon tire, and Leeder and Faith could speed past him.

However, 'C' would never quit, and his sheer determination and big heart always kept him in the race. Leeder and Faith knew it was only a matter of time before the big rhino would actually win a race with them, and they would have to listen to his ribbing for days thereafter. So after each race, Leeder would laugh and say "Not today, big boy, not today," and Faith would kiss 'C's massive horn and say, with a smile, "We only beat you by a nose."

The big rhino was the first to begin a race, start a fight, lead an adventure, or tell a joke. He was fearless, if sometimes impulsive, and he had a face that made you love him and want to be around him, horns and all.

Faith, on the other hand, was always there when you needed her. She never started a race or a fight or an adventure. She couldn't tell a joke if her life depended on it. But she always made sense out of whatever they did. She was consistent. It was almost as if nothing seemed the same without her, and she could find meaning and purpose in the most mundane happenings.

Leeder looked at his two longtime friends, and said, "You just can't be too careful when you are this far away from the herd you know. It can be dangerous."

They each looked at one another and laughed. The day appeared almost perfect. So the three of them rolled in the grass, ate, and played for what seemed like hours.

The rest of the antelope herd was now up and foraging the tender grass as if they had not eaten in days. They were far away from Leeder and his friends, remaining near the trees and cloistered with hundreds, moving and eating like one giant family.

Beyond the antelope was a herd of zebra calling to each other with sounds so distant Leeder could hardly hear them. The zebra were fast and had powerful rear legs, but Leeder's mother had always told him the zebra talked a great deal but did little to help the herd.

It was cooler near the trees, but dark and mysterious as well. The herd was always loath to enter the thicket but curious about the eyes that leered at them from the edges as well as the noise and activity they heard inside. The unknown was never good for the herd, and in the minds of most herd members the thicket was filled with the unknown.

Within the trees, the Douts were running everywhere. They were gray monkeys with white chests, small eyes, and long tails. They varied in size but their powerful tails allowed even the smallest to clinch and hold fast to almost anything if they were given the time to attach themselves. They made it their business to be everywhere. They had a unique way of being nowhere and everywhere at the same time, and they thrived on listening to the conversations of the other animals and offering their uninvited commentaries.

One family trait that seemed ever present with the Douts was their negativism. No one had ever met a Dout who was optimistic about anything. Perhaps they were justified because history had no record of any Dout ever being successful at anything.

The smaller Douts moved so fast they seemed to walk on all fours. The bigger Douts were slower and stronger choosing to walk only on their rear legs and to use their mighty arm strength to wrestle position and retain it. They spent most of their time lounging in the trees, and though they appeared to be asleep, they were always watching and waiting for opportunities to influence the outcome of a situation.

But out in the sun-filled grasslands, far from any Douts and the mystery of the tree thicket, the hot sun was now slowly making its way into the afternoon sky. Leeder, 'C,' and Faith continued to tumble and play, all the while feeling inside that life was good and their future as bright as the splashes of sun illuminating their playground.

Suddenly, the air seemed to change. It was not a change in the wind or the temperature. No clouds were moving in. But something was dramatically different. It was the kind of change animals could sense. Not with their eyes, or their ears. Not with their touch. But the three friends sensed it together without speaking. It was the sense of fear's quietness rolling in smoothly across the grass and deafening all joy in its wake. It was a sense they could not and should not ignore.

"The Killers!" shrieked Leeder. "Run!"

Without debate, the three friends bolted to find the herd. They had never seen the Killers, but they had seen their handiwork. They had walked past the skeletal remains of their savage attacks, and they had always been warned by the other herd members to never look, just keep walking. There was much they did not know about this dread, but this much they knew too well: the Killers meant death.

Unfortunately, the three had strayed so far they could not see the herd over the tall grass and the wind was blowing in the wrong direction to pick up the herd's scent. In the distance, Leeder could make out the top of the trees to the south of the herd so he shouted, "Run to the trees!"

As they ran to find the herd, Leeder became more and more afraid. How could he have been so foolish? What if it was not the Killers, would he look silly? Why did he ever leave the herd?

As usual, 'C' had left first but tired quickly. Leeder passed him and continued to run. He paid no attention to the fact that he could no longer sense the presence of either 'C' or Faith. The fear within Leeder had now firmly taken control, and it was directing every ounce of his energy to the muscles driving his legs with one order: run from the Killers. He remembered what he had been taught: run from the Killers, run, just run and get to the herd. There was no time to wait for 'C' or Faith to catch up, no time to turn his head to find them. Survival became his only goal and that meant finding the herd.

As he continued running for the treetops, he heard the faint sound of a familiar voice calling his name so he turned towards it as he continued his desperate scramble. With each step the voice became more discernable, and then he saw her. His mother was pacing up and down near the herd's edge, far out in the grassland and still well away from the trees.

"Leeder, where have you been? I was so worried."

"Mother, the Killers, I think the Killers are coming!"

"I know, son, where is Faith?"

"I… I don't know. I guess I was so afraid, I lost her when I started running. I don't know where 'C' is either."

"That boy! He gets you into more trouble."

"But Mother, it was not 'C's fault. I wanted to go."

"Well, at least you're safe now, just stay with the herd. It's going to be dangerous for awhile."

Anne was Leeder's mother. She was well respected in the herd and had already raised several other children who had taken their places as herd members. She got along well with the other animals including the rhinos and had been instrumental in developing the friendship between Leeder, 'C,' and Faith. She never said much, but when she did everyone took her seriously. They knew that she was a bit formal and a stickler for following the herd rules. If Anne did something, everyone knew it was herd policy and you could follow her lead. Leeder was her youngest, and although she knew he would soon be on his own, he still had a special place in her heart.

As Leeder moved into the large herd he could not help but worry about 'C' and Faith. Were they okay? Had the Killers found them?

He began asking the other animals if any of them had seen 'C' or Faith, but they were all so nervous and worried about their own safety that they merely brushed him aside. One older female antelope even snapped at him and screamed, "Mind your own business! Don't you know the Killers are coming?"

As he stepped back to avoid the thrust of her bite, he heard a deep piercing screech.

"Watch it, Leeder! Just because that old cow tried to take your head off doesn't mean you have to step on mine!"

It was Sid. Everybody knew Sid. He was an old vulture with white hair on top and a tuxedo-like body of feathers on the bottom. He was always dressed formally even though his feathers constantly seemed a bit disheveled. He was an undertaker, and while no one wanted to partake of his services, they knew he had a job to do.

Sid had a terrible sense of smell which was an asset in his profession, but he had keen eyes and not much went past him. He attended all the events and everyone liked him because he made them all feel as if they were his best friend. His parting words were normally, "Remember, you're my best bud." He knew all the gossip and was willing to trade all he knew for any new morsel of information you could tell him. Nothing brought a well concealed smile to his face like hearing a report that one of the animals was sick or dead.

"Just want to pay my condolences," he would say, always making it clear that he was just there to "clean up everybody else's mess."

"What are you doing here Sid?" Leeder asked. "I thought you were still in charge of that large branch in the trees."

"It's a jungle in there boy. Everybody is panicked over this Killer thing. Word is, this is where the action will be, and I just want to be ready in case my services are needed."

Sid leaned in conspiratorially, "Now, did I hear you ask that old antelope about 'C' and Faith?"

"Yes, I lost them in the grassland. The last time I saw them we were running toward the trees because we could not find the herd," said Leeder. "I'm really starting to worry about them."

"I saw them both heading into the trees a short while ago when I was flying here. You know me, I don't like to get into other folks' business, but it looked like they were looking for something or somebody."

"Probably me…," Leeder confessed as his eyes surveyed the area for any sign of 'C' or Faith.

"Well I tell you, not that you asked, but those trees are no place for a stupid rhino and a silly girl if the Killers are coming. Oh well, I guess it's good for business."

"Don't say that, Sid!" Leeder snapped. "They are my best friends."

"Were your best friends, you mean. Trust me. I've seen it all in my years. If you don't look out for number one, nobody else will. I know. I've made a career out of fools and heroes. It doesn't matter to me which they are. When they go it alone, I get the business. If your friends are in those trees away from the herd when the Killers come, there will be work for me to do."

Leeder looked at Sid and pleaded, "Sid, you know far more about the thicket than I do. It is so big. How could anyone ever find them if they are in there? How could they find their way out?"

"Find old Mr. Wisdom. He has lived there longer than anyone I know. If they are there, he will know."

Sid was in a hurry to get a look at the rest of the herd and clearly had no patience for further questions. So he looked up at Leeder and said, "Remember Leeder, your family is special to me. You're my best bud. If those friends of yours… you know… if there is anything I can do… if they can use my services just give me a call." With that, Sid swooped away to check the condition of the other animals.

Leeder stared at the trees that were only a few hundred yards away. He could get there quickly, but it was dangerous. If the Killers caught an antelope in the trees his agility would be reduced. The brief time it took to dodge a tree or clump of brush could be the difference between escape and being caught in the Killers' grasp. Yet, he could not live with himself knowing he had abandoned "C" and Faith. What if he never saw them again? What if they went into the thicket looking for him? After all, he had told them to run for the trees initially before his mother's voice helped him find the herd.

Leeder made his way to the edge of the herd. He paused, and then he stepped into the open grass. Before he knew it he was racing towards the trees. He could hear his mother and other members of the herd calling, but still he ran. As he reached the tree line he cautiously snorted at the ground debating his fears. But he had come too far now, time was running out. He stepped inside.

It was dark. The Douts were everywhere and even around his feet. They tried to attach themselves to his legs, but he instinctively brushed them away. He asked them if they had seen a rhino or an antelope come through recently.

"They didn't climb the tree," proclaimed one of the smaller Douts.

"They didn't go back in the grassland," said another.

"Aren't you worried about the Killers?" three of them shouted in a chorus.

"Don't listen to them, son, they love to tell you where not to go, but they are not very good at telling you where to go," Leeder heard someone say.

Leeder looked up on a branch extending from a large old tree directly in front of him and saw a rather distinguished owl preening himself as he gazed at Leeder.

"Are you Mr. Wisdom?" Leeder asked.

"Heavens no!" replied the owl. "I'm called Messenger."

"Have you seen my friends?" Leeder pleaded.

"No."

"Then I do not suppose you can help me."

"Sure I can." Messenger stated rather optimistically.

"How?"

"I can tell you where they are."

"How can you do that if you haven't seen them?" Leeder quipped with a puzzled look.

"Everybody that comes in here gets lost at first, but if they don't give up they end up finding the road."

"What road?"

"The road to old Mr. Wisdom's place."

"How do you know that's where they are?" Leeder asked as he peered suspiciously at Messenger.

"You obviously did not see them on your way in or you would not have entered. Likewise, you do not see them on that wide path over there do you?"

Leeder glanced at the well-worn path just off to his right, then responded back to Messenger, "No."

"Then your friends have not quit. If they have not quit, then they must be on the road. The quitters always end up on that path over there. That is why it is known as Quitter's Path."

"How do I find this Mr. Wisdom's place?" asked Leeder.

"You have to find the road," replied Messenger.

"Then for goodness sake, where is the road?" Leeder questioned with exasperation.

"Just keep walking… it'll find you. It is not as complicated as you might think."

Leeder was frustrated but he knew he was running out of time. He began walking through the dark trees, lowering his head to avoid the branches and using his horns to push through the thick brush. If the Killers attacked now his speed would be useless because there was no place to run. His strength was no match for the Killers.

He had become so used to the Douts following him around that he almost forgot they were still there. They began pulling at his legs and reminding him of the Quitters Path just behind them. They suggested that if he left now, he could get back to the herd in time. 'C' and Faith were probably already there they argued.

Leeder pressed on. And then he saw it. Not much of a road really, more like a trail but he was excited to see it. He moved down it faster and faster, and then he saw a small clearing where a number of animals had gathered including Faith and 'C.'

He was elated just to find them alive, and quickly moved to his friends and asked, "'C,' Faith, are you all right?"

"We are now," replied Faith.

"But how did you both get here?" Leeder inquired.

"We were looking for you and hoped you would find us here," Faith answered. "We have been listening to Mr. Wisdom, and he has been telling us the most fascinating things."

Leeder looked up above Faith's head and saw the same proud owl he met when he first entered the thicket, now perched on the large branch directly in front of Faith. He was still preening himself and paid little attention to Leeder's arrival.

"I thought you were Mr. Wisdom all the time," Leeder cried out to the owl who sat passively with no response.

"But Leeder, that's not Mr. Wisdom," Faith said softly.

"Well who is?" Leeder asked.

"I am," responded a large old tortoise sitting in the corner who Leeder had mistaken for an ugly rock when he first arrived.

Leeder seemed speechless as he could only utter, "But... but."

"But I do not look very much like Wisdom. Is that what you are trying to say?" said the old turtle as he straightened his neck, turned his head, and looked squarely into Leeder's eyes.

"I have learned through the years that people often listen to my words more when I speak through folks like Messenger here. More often than not they confuse him with me just as you did. I really do not care as long as they listen, and right now you need very much to listen," Mr. Wisdom said with more authority than Leeder had ever heard.

"Your friends have been telling me much about you, and I have come to conclude that you are fortunate to have such good companions. Friends like these are hard to find, and I would keep them close if I were you."

"Have you heard about the Killers?" Leeder asked.

"Yes."

"Yet you don't seem afraid."

"I am not. Over the years those who have tried to destroy me have always failed."

Faith interrupted, "Leeder you need to listen to what Mr. Wisdom has to say about the Killers."

"Have you ever seen them?" asked Leeder.

"No, but I know what they look like."

"But how, I don't understand…?"

Old Mr. Wisdom slowly lifted his eyebrows and turned his wrinkled head slightly to the branch above his head. "My good friend, Messenger, does my seeing sometimes as well."

Messenger continued to sit quietly on the branch content to survey the happening without comment.

The number of smaller Douts seemed to be growing. They were now all over 'C' and Faith, and they were getting more and more restless. Suddenly, Leeder heard a tremendous roar that literally shook the ground upon which they were standing.

"What was that?" 'C' shouted.

"It is beginning," said Mr. Wisdom.

* * *

The Killers had begun to take their positions in the grasslands. The male Killer was the key to the attack. He was almost six hundred pounds of solid muscle which he proudly displayed with each movement of his enormous body. Despite his size, he moved with stealth through the high grass almost unnoticeable. His thick mane and glimmering coat drew attention away from the battle scars on his hip and shoulders, which he wore like badges of honor from previous campaigns. Each step was slow, calculated, machine-like. He picked his way through the thickness until he found a large open patch in the grass several hundred feet long.

This was where he would direct the battle. This now became his sacred territory for no other animal would be foolish enough to challenge him. Here he sat, for he was too proud to crouch. He waited. Confident that time was on his side and that his very presence evoked fear, the great lion knew he would control the beginning and the end of this engagement.

Far to the rear of the grassland moved the female Killers. They were sleek, lean, powerful, and faster than the male. These lionesses were the real hunters. They too were patient as each of the twelve of them moved quietly into position. Now they would wait, wait for the Roar.

No one knew the name of the great lion. No one dared to ask. They only knew that he was the personification of the roar that identified him and the fear that went before him. He was the Roar, and the Roar was him.

The Roar could be heard for more than six miles. The lionesses had done this before, and although it was mid-afternoon, they knew the Roar often liked the battle to be near twilight when the light favored the hunter. Darkness was death's friend, and they were happy to await its arrival.

When the Roar began, the hunted animals would frighten easily. Each of the animals would hear it differently, but they would hear it, and they would feel the fear it proclaimed. Let the fear work, the lionesses thought, it would make the attack easier.

They had watched before and knew that as the Roar intensified so would the panic. The lionesses would move closer to the Roar as the other animals were moving away from it. Patience was their virtue and their weapon. If fear did its work and paralyzed their prey, the synchronized forward movement of the lionesses would entrap the hunted like a giant invisible net. If they ran from the Roar, the lionesses would be ready and death would come quickly. Either way, the trap was set.

The Roar had begun. It was time to slowly close the trap.

* * *

Back at Wisdom's place, 'C' asked, "The beginning of what?"

"The beginning of the Roar," responded Wisdom.

"What will happen?" Faith implored.

"The Roar will become greater and the Killers will come," said Wisdom.

Leeder thought about his mother, his family, the rest of the herd. Then it was his turn to move in and look Wisdom in the eye. Leeder then pleaded, "Is there anything I can do?"

Wisdom replied, "Run to the Roar."

Leeder had been so focused on his conversation with Wisdom that he had failed to notice the arrival of two larger Douts who had slipped in unnoticed and taken their places.

"Yeah that's right, kid, run to the roar. Run to your death is what he should be saying. There's a six hundred pound lion out there who would just love to have you over for dinner. Why don't you just run to the roar? Better yet, ask the old fellow if he has ever run to the roar," interjected the particularly unkempt and overweight Dout as he stood up from his seat.

Leeder looked at Wisdom, "Have you ever run to the roar?"

"No," responded the unapologetic Mr. Wisdom.

"Then why are you telling me to do it?" said Leeder.

"I'm not telling anyone what to do. I was asked if there was anything you could do. There is. You can Run to the Roar!"

The other larger Dout was now on his feet and trying to assert himself by saying, "Why don't you tell the little kid what you are doing? You're sending him to his death!"

Wisdom fired back, "I'm sending him to his destiny."

Faith quietly moved between the two larger Douts and Leeder. She then softly asked Wisdom, "What should he do?"

Wisdom once again looked at Leeder and said, "The years have not shown me whether the times are made for us or we are made for the times, but I know this: there are moments in life when the two overlap and the success of our lives is determined by the choices we make during those moments."

"This ain't your moment kid, leave that to the heroes," the first Dout replied.

'C' stepped up, "Leeder what about your Mom and the rest of the herd?"

Messenger who had been flying in and out landed on the branch once again and looked down to say with a new nervousness, "The moment is here. Choose."

Wisdom in a voice so soft Leeder could hardly hear repeated, "Choose."

'C' then bulled his way to the front and said, "I say we go!"

One of the smaller Douts had succeeded in getting its tail locked around Leeder's front leg. The first larger Dout put his arm around Leeder's neck and said, "You're not going anywhere. If the Killers go after the herd then so be it. They will not get them all. But if they see you coming out of here they may come back looking for us."

Messenger pleaded this time in an even more urgent voice, "Time! Time! You must choose!"

The Roars came faster… louder.

Wisdom spoke up, "Quickly! You must go! To your right are two paths. They both lead out. The wider one leads back to the herd, the narrow one to the Roar. Choose well, Leeder. Remember, the moments of life pass but once, the choices we make within them revisit us for a lifetime."

Leeder knew he had to get out of the trees no matter which way he went, but the Douts made it difficult to move.

'C' turned abruptly and charged for the narrow path which had become somewhat overgrown with vines and thistles as a result of years of disuse. But they were no match for the powerful rhino who hit with such force that they were knocked away, opening the trail for the others.

As he did, Faith turned and with all her might kicked the first large Dout in the chest with such force that he needed both hands to keep from falling. His arm left Leeder's neck, and Leeder lunged for the narrow path's entrance. As he bolted through, the smaller Dout, still wrapped around his leg, hit the edge of a large tree and was flung off into the brush. The second large Dout dove towards the path and reached to grab Leeder's hind leg, but Faith was right behind him and her well-placed hoof in the palm of the Dout's hand ensured that he would not be in the grabbing business for a while.

'C' was barreling down the path, clearing it for Leeder and Faith as they ran faster and faster toward the light. When they cleared the tree line, Leeder could tell 'C' was slowing down as usual. He knew it was his turn to move to the front so he focused his eyes, tightened his nostrils, lowered his head and did what he did best: he ran.

The grass was too tall for him to see with his head down, but if he held it up he could not run as fast. He needed the speed so he lowered his head and Ran to the Roar. He knew he did not want to lose 'C' or Faith again as he had done earlier, so as he ran he continued to call their names. Perhaps they would hear his voice and they would Run to the Roar together, but he had chosen to run and there was no turning back. Leeder also knew that Wisdom had told him to "Run to the Roar," but even Wisdom could not describe what he would find when he arrived. That was his destiny, and it had yet to be written.

In the distance, Anne saw the movement through the grass and recognized Leeder's voice. She knew the Killers might be near. She knew they might be after Leeder. But this was her son and she knew she must do what she could to help him. So she ran after Leeder's voice.

Her quick jolt startled the other members of the herd who mistook her actions as the signal for the herd's movement. Certainly Anne would never do anything but obey the rules of the herd. If Anne was moving, it must be time for all of them to move. They must have missed the signal. It was time to run. Soon hundreds of antelope were on the move, not knowing where they were going but following Anne as she followed her son's voice.

The zebras and the other rhinos saw the fuss and joined what they thought was an escape, not even realizing they were running toward the Roar rather than away from it. Soon the pounding of hundreds of hooves created a cloud of dust so great that no one knew which direction they were running, they just followed the body in front of them. The pounding was also echoing in their ears and distorting the sound of the Roar until it was almost impossible for the herd to tell the direction from which it was coming or even if it had stopped.

The lionesses in the rear were puzzled. Why were the animals all running toward the Roar? Yet, they did not dare leave their posts. The Roar would turn them around. He always did. They would be back soon. The lionesses had to wait.

Leeder continued to run. The sun seemed much hotter than before and the sweat on his forehead was streaming into his eyes and causing them to burn. His nostrils were flaring in an attempt to get as much oxygen as possible into his straining lungs, and he knew that if a single hoof landed in an unnoticed hole in the ground he could be brought to his knees. Leeder knew a broken leg to an antelope was a death sentence.

Finally, Leeder stopped calling the names of Faith and 'C.' He knew he had to run with all his might even if he had to run alone.

He also knew he had to concentrate, he had to focus. So he lifted his head proudly to show his horns and see across the grass. As he did, he felt a bump on his left shoulder and glanced to see Faith running side by side with him, her shoulder even with his, each blending their strides as if they were one.

"I'm here Leeder. I've been here all the time. We will Run to the Roar together," said Faith still in her quiet yet comforting voice.

The next step carried Leeder into the clear patch of grass where for the first time he saw the Roar off to his right. Their eyes locked. Leeder felt his knees weaken slightly and then heard Faith's voice again, "Don't look, just keep going Leeder. Keep running."

The Killer was shocked at the sudden sight of the two antelope galloping across his stronghold. He instinctively lurched from his sitting position to all fours and then also noticed the large cloud of dust in the distance coming his way from the stampeding herd, but he could not discern what it was. This had never happened before. Everything was going in the wrong direction.

Though not accustomed to being the sole killer, the Roar knew he could not let the two antelope pass. Despite the fact the hunt had not gone exactly as planned, a kill was still a kill. With agility unmatched by any other creature his size the Roar turned, his powerful hind legs drove into the ground and then launched him towards Leeder.

Within seconds he was within range of Leeder's neck and ready to close the attack. With one last mighty roar he sprang as his jaw opened wide revealing rows of sharpened teeth ready to end Leeder's life.

Focused on his kill's neck, the Roar never saw the pile of dust coming on Leeder's right flank with the speed of a gazelle and the grace of a…well really without much grace at all. It came like a torpedo, but this time the Roar was the target.

Still focused on the kill, the lion never heard the deep voice reverberating from the cloud of dust saying, "Not today, my friend, not today. You don't outrun old Courage today!"

The huge lion never saw 'C' as he dipped his head and drove his large front horn square into the Roar's chest with such power that the two were driven to the ground spinning over twice. Somehow, miraculously, 'C's momentum kept him moving forward landing back on his stocky legs which had never stopped running.

The Roar had neither seen nor heard 'C', but he now felt the power of Courage. The lion was stunned and disoriented. As he futilely tried to move his massive body, it was too late. The herd came storming over him not able to stop even if that had been their desire. They came and came not knowing why or even how. They just kept coming for almost an hour until the last of them had crossed the clearing. And then, just as quickly as they had started, the herd stopped running.

Several miles back, the lionesses watched the sun lowering in the sky but no longer could hear the Roar. What could possibly have ended the Roar they wondered? They watched each other, then slowly one by one they left and scattered in different directions. This day was done.

While the dust was settling, Leeder, Faith, and 'C' looked at the herd which was now grazing almost as if nothing had happened. Faith walked over to Courage and kissed his big wonderful head.

"What?" asked Courage with a sheepish smile on his face.

"I just wanted you to know how much you mean to Leeder and me you big hunk of whatever you are," said Faith.

Just then Sid came swooping in with his normal bluster and landed on the back of Courage.

"Get off me you old vulture," Courage said as he looked around at Sid still standing on one of his humps.

"Sorry to disappoint you, Sid, but the Roar needs you today, not us. I kind of thought you would be over there taking care of things," Leeder added.

"I'm letting my boys handle that one. I've been checking out the rest of the herd. Seems like everybody is in good shape. There's a lot of talk going around you know. The herd's thinking about putting in some kind of new policy, something about 'Running to the Roar.' You guys have really shaken things up. I wouldn't even be surprised if folks are talking about this for a long time to come. Oh well, I've got to fly. The Douts are fighting with each other again and my services might be needed. Anyway, just remember you are all my best buds."

Leeder, Faith, and Courage smiled as Sid took off. The sky was growing darker with the twilight moving in. No more words were spoken. None were needed. The three friends realized how much they needed each other. They also realized the day had not turned out like they had planned, but life was good and the sun would announce a new day tomorrow.

They did not know what that new day would bring, nor for that matter the ones that would follow it. But they did know they would forever remember that on this day, this special day, they had Run to the Roar.

Sid turned out to be correct. The animals did tell this story for a long time and they passed it down from generation to generation. The younger animals reenacted the scene time and again, each wanting to play the part of Leeder, Faith, or Courage. Courage was never called 'C' again.

It is well known that from that day until animals spoke no more, the first member of the herd who Ran to the Roar was always referred to as "Leeder." It is equally well known that of those who earned the title "Leeder," the most successful were always the ones who ran with the inspiration of Faith and the strength of Courage at their side.

As for Mr. Wisdom, well he continued to give sound advice through Messenger for as long as anyone could remember, and there are those who say he continues today. In fact, when the fears of life roar loudest, when the night is darkest, and when hope seems but yesterday's memory, anyone who seeks him with the simple question, "Is there anything I can do?" can still hear the voice of Wisdom saying softly through one of his Messengers, "***Run To The Roar.***"

Afterword

Can you hear the roars around you? They are all around growing louder. More and more of us feel discouraged or paralyzed by the sounds of fear. Not unlike the Killer's roar in the preceding fable, we each hear them differently, but they are heard nonetheless. Some hear the anxiousness in a plummeting economy, some the apparent hopelessness of a medical report, and others the uncertainty of a world changing so fast they can hardly find their place. Each situation is different, but the outcome is always the same: the fear itself threatens to destroy us.

As I was discussing this with my good friend Rolfe Carawan, he retold me an illustration he uses in one of his signature keynotes about the method lions use to hunt. It was out of that conversation that the *Run to the Roar Fable* was born.

One evening shortly after I penned the final revisions for the *Run to the Roar Fable,* I was walking past a diner, half-empty following the dinner rush. I found myself stopped on the sidewalk peering in the window imagining some of the people with whom I had recently counseled were eating supper inside.

Seated by the window was a smiling young couple. Near them was a family with two children in high chairs. A booth towards the back held two women who by the similarities of their faces I could tell were a mother and her grown daughter. And in the center of the restaurant an elderly couple sat quietly enjoying supper.

On the surface, the occupants of each table seemed content, even happy. But underneath I knew another story.

It was now six months since the smiling young man at the front of the diner had started looking for a job. He had such high hopes when he graduated with one of the first college degrees in his family. He had even kept his spirits up during the first three months as he enthusiastically passed out resumes and hoped for a return phone call or even an email. But now, with student loans looming and not even an interview on the horizon, he was beginning to lose confidence. These days he tried to keep smiling in front of his dinner date who he hoped one day would become his wife. Even then though, for the first time in his young life he was beginning to fear his future, not embrace it.

The young family nearby was not just juggling the demands of two young children at dinnertime. While they kept their hands busy feeding and tidying the spills of the toddlers at the table, their minds were busy juggling other demands. Things had been going so well just months before. The father had even kept his job during the first round of layoffs at the plant. But then came the bills from an unexpected medical emergency, the interest rate on their home had adjusted, and the plant cut hours back for all the remaining employees. They had started making ends meet by using their credit cards. Now, no matter how many sleepless nights they spent reworking their budget, they couldn't figure out how to pay their bills. They were quickly approaching the limits on their credit cards. The broken stove waiting at home would max them out. How then would they pay their mortgage? There was a time when they would have enjoyed eating out as a family. Getting those times back seemed impossible now.

At the booth in the back, the waitress had just delivered two plates of chicken cordon bleu. It was her mother's favorite. She had hoped that taking Mom to dinner tonight would spark a glimmer of the woman that she had known growing up. But her mother's empty gaze hadn't faded. Ever since the divorce, the depression seemed to get worse by the day. Some days Mom didn't even get out of bed. She knew it ran in families, but didn't dare let on her suspicion that she herself might be suffering from depression too.

In the center of the diner the elderly couple had finished their meal and was now just quietly sipping decaffeinated coffee. Normally, at this time in the evening he would be strolling down the sidewalk with his wife on his arm on their weekly window-shopping tour of the local antique shops. It was a tradition they had rarely missed in their forty-nine years of marriage. In fact, the only times he could remember not taking that stroll was during some of life's most special milestones – the birth of their son, the day they welcomed their daughter into the world, the family road trip out West, the marriages of their children, and finally the births of their four beautiful grandchildren. Today's milestone was different from all the others though. Just hours before he had received the diagnosis. They could treat the cancer, the doctor said, but it would likely only prolong his life by six months – maybe enough time for the 50th anniversary party his children were planning. But maybe not.

Across America and throughout the world, people are facing all sorts of challenges. I think about these people on nearly a daily basis and the struggles that stare at them, and paralyze them with fear. Imagine how their lives could be transformed if they Ran to the Roar. Imagine how our families, and our communities, and our nation would be transformed if we Ran to the Roar. Whatever diner, café or coffee shop you are sitting in, whatever challenges you are facing, you have a choice. Imagine if you Ran to the Roar.

J. Randy Forbes

More About the Authors

Randy Forbes, as a member of the United States Congress, founded and chaired the Congressional Prayer Caucus, the China Caucus, and the Modeling & Simulation Caucus. His willingness to Run to the Roar is perhaps best exemplified by the fact that he is one of a very few individuals to have been honored with the highest civilian award offered by both the United States Army and the United States Navy. Randy Forbes graduated valedictorian from Randolph-Macon College and received his law degree from the University of Virginia School of Law. He and his wife Shirley live in Chesapeake, Virginia. They have four children: Neil, Jamie, Jordan, and Justin.

Rolfe Carawan, founder of Carawan Global Group, is a speaker, coach and consultant for leaders and organizations around the world. Dedicated to his personal mission to "relieve suffering and release potential," for nearly two decades he has collaborated with leaders and their teams to increase productivity and bottom-line results through the development of healthy work cultures, unified teams and principled leadership. Committed to bringing real solutions, his timeless messages have impacted small and mid-size businesses, Fortune 500 companies, churches and educational organizations, professional and medical practices. Rolfe and Lea, married since 1987, have two children, Drew and Rachel. His commitment to Running to the Roar is best shown in that he and Lea have partnered in business for over 20 years and lived to tell about it. Visit him on the web at www. RolfeCarawan.com.

We invite you to learn more about Run to the Roar and to contact us at www.RunToTheRoar.com.

9 781600 376047